Santo and I

Gavin Stolten
Illustrated by Marjorie Scott

My name is Paco.

Santo is my grandson.

We live in Greenvale.

I've lived here since I was little.

Sometimes Santo and I walk down
Main Street together.

I remember what Main Street was like
when I was little.

Sometimes I take Santo to the park.

I remember what the park was like
when I was little.

Sometimes Santo and I go to the lake together.

I remember what the lake was like
when I was little.

Sometimes I take Santo to school.

I remember what the school was like
when I was little.

Sometimes Santo and I go to a baseball game together.

I remember what baseball games were like
when I was little.

Sometimes Santo and I help in the hardware store.

I remember what the store was like
when Santo's dad was little.